my first

Preschool

ABC

Picture Book

This book belongs to:

_____

A is for
Art

B is for Books

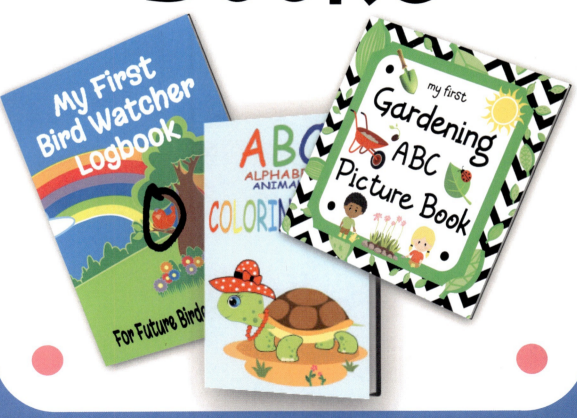

C is for
Cubbies

E is for
Easel

F is for

Friends

G is for
Globe

H is for
Health

I is for
Inclusivity

J is for
Janitor

K is for
Keyboard

L is for
Library

N is for
Notebook

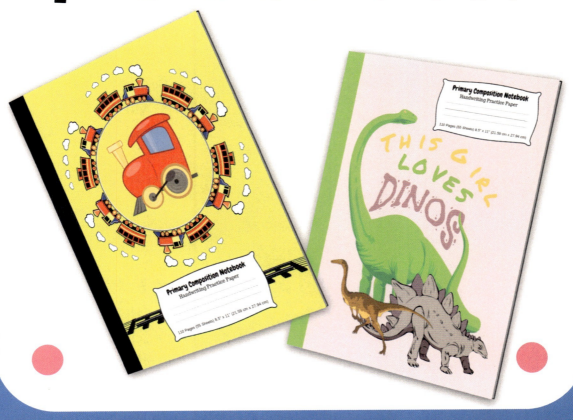

O is for
Online Class

P is for
Puzzles

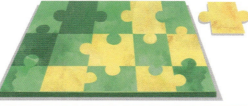

Q is for Questions

R is for
Recess

S is for
School

T is for
Teacher

U is for
Umbrella

V is for
Vehicle

W is for
Writing

X is for
Xylophone

Y is for
Yardstick

Made in the USA
Middletown, DE
02 September 2022